I0797942

INFINITE AUDITION

INFINITE AUDITION

Charlie Petch

Brick Books

Library and Archives Canada Cataloguing in Publication

Title: Infinite audition / Charlie Petch.
Names: Petch, Charlie, author
Identifiers: Canadiana (print) 20250212935 | Canadiana (ebook) 20250213133 | ISBN 9781771316552 (softcover) | ISBN 9781771316576 (PDF) | ISBN 9781771316569 (EPUB)
Subjects: LCGFT: Spoken word poetry.
Classification: LCC PS8631.E815 I54 2026 | DDC C811/.6—dc23

We gratefully acknowledge the Canada Council for the Arts, the Government of Canada through the Canada Book Fund, the Ontario Arts Council, and the Government of Ontario for their support of our publishing program.

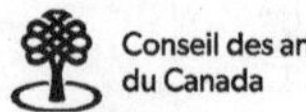

Edited by Sonnet L'Abbé
Author photo by Nika Belianina
Cover and interior design by Emmie Tsumura

Brick Books
487 King St. W.
Kingston, ON
K7L 2X7
www.brickbooks.ca

Though much of the work of Brick Books takes place on the ancestral lands of the Anishinaabeg, Haudenosaunee, Huron-Wendat, and Mississaugas of the Credit peoples, our editors, authors, and readers from many back-grounds are situated from coast to coast to coast in Canada on the traditional and unceded territories of over six hundred nations who have cared for Turtle Island from time immemorial. While living and working on these lands, we are committed to hearing and returning the rightful imaginative space to the poetries, songs, and stories that have been untold, under-told, wrongly told, and suppressed through colonization.

Table of Contents

Act I: We Can Be a Different Man
Poems for Solo Performance

Act II: All Horns and Drums and Triumphant Strings
Poems to Be Performed with Music or Puppetry

Act I:
We Can Be a Different Man

Poems for Solo Performance

Good News

My gender is a party crasher
it's the television show you'd never admit watching
it's the tampon that wanted a different life

it's a piece of spinach
stuck in teeth
that grew so big
it pushed a molar out
it's a mouthful of blood
in polite conversation
it's why some of you
stopped listening

or maybe we don't know
good news when we hear it
anymore

aren't we artists?
don't we make dresses
out of war propaganda films?
don't we plant tiny explosions
called *revolution*
called *think different*
called *let's keep this going*
        until we get this right

coming out trans
is a slow avalanche
as I try to celebrate

like I saved a life
like I saved my life
like I stopped my infinite
audition to be a woman

like look at my happy
but all people seem to hear
are boulders dropping out of my mouth
    they/them/he/him
    transmasculine

is there an app I can use?
some sort of google translator
that can make people hear this
as good news?

because it feels
like I'm telling people
my best friend
is alive again

I don't let him go this time

as rocks fall from our mouth
as people turn and flee
my male self asks me
    how was the hiding
    what you did
    to be called one of the guys?

I ask him to hold me
to pull me from that mud

tell him how I missed him
and now that he's really here
we can be a different man
be our own man
thanks to slow avalanches
like art
like unafraid

I tell him
I'm so sorry
I ever thought
I could bury you
you have always been
my good news

Trans March 2022

The newly-out pandemic trans are here
puppy energy is everywhere
their first time in community
the march ends in Allan Gardens
I dance to the bands as much as I
search for those who will remember
who we lost
search for those
who survived

I marched with my newfound sister
we were once in a cowboy band
handed our old drag to each other
now I joke that the band will listen to me
but not to her
we laugh and cope and shine

I feel the vertigo of two-and-a-half years
of lockdowns   of missing this space that's ours
this joy of feeling normal
it only happens in each other's company
I can't leave this park where we gather
until the last trans has left

the pull of trans space makes me forget my safety
I lose track of my sister and the party vanishes
I take my pride beads off my neck slide them

into backpack my movement a honed reflex
an attempt to disappear
so that I don't

leaving the house as ourselves is political
trans people are always marching
in the boots and heels and wheels of our ancestors
I used to feel like an abandoned alien
until the revolution of us
finally found me

It's Me, Your Closet

Hey look
In case you were wondering
(and I see that you're not)
your closet is doing just
fine without you

yeah I mean who needs
to hear all that crying and
wailing and I really got
sick of hearing "Toxic" on
repeat I mean Britney does
have other songs

I don't care that
I'm no longer the only one
who knows your true form
the specialness of what
we had was clearly just foreplay
I was merely a launch pad for
the jet plane of your
sexuality and identity

I have your pronouns down though
I've been practising them with
you for years all those speeches
for your parents I have them memorized
how was it telling them?
you never came back to say

ok I know I know I don't
represent a refuge to you anymore
I guess at some point I have to
accept I was more of a prison-cell-type metaphor
but really I'm just four walls
some hangers
and a light switch

are you sure you don't
need me anymore?
I mean grandma's coming
next week

I loved our every moment
sometimes I flick the lights
on and off when you walk by
I put the fake fur carpet askew
I just want you to notice me

I'm not doing ok really
I'm all for the revolution
I'm here for your happiness
as much as I held your sadness

I never wanted to stifle you
I just wanted to keep you safe
like any small room should

I'm just saying
maybe you should tear me down
and reconstruct me into the dollhouse

you always wanted
one that is all dressing rooms
and boudoirs and no need to hide
I don't want to be a closet anymore
I don't want anyone to find me
crawl inside
and almost

disappear

Chronic Immune Thrombocytopenic Purpura

The world moves on
            and I'm still bleeding
the masks come off
            and I'm still bleeding
my partner moves on
            and I'm still bleeding
some friends fall away
            and I'm still bleeding

it's so easy to just let
it all go just let litres of
type B positive thoughts
and handfuls of clots
drop from my body

I'm taking coagulants
with molly expectations
and sometimes it lets
me go for a day or two
we are so new to being in public again
no one asks
where have you been?

my bed is a bloodletting
my hugs are blood pressure cuffs
my outings are iron infusions
blood labs waiting rooms and pharmacies

my gender becomes a spectre
that haunts me in mirrors
as I check below eyelids to see
if my deadname on my health card
needs a transfusion

some part of me is falling down
some part of me thinks it's yesterday
and everything is too low to the ground
to get back up again and I
swoon when I turn around and they tell me
the pandemic is over but all I do
is try to not need the emergency room
because I was just there
and it was the loneliest I'd
ever felt in a crowd

like maybe
I'd die and everyone would just
move up in line over top of me

I can't blame them I used
to work here and it's a different
morality

but they say
the pandemic's over
so why all the coughing and intubating?

Maybe if I say
the bleeding is over
do you think it will stop?

Photophobia

After a migraine that became
a monster that ate my brain
I now have these short little seizures
when lights flicker and flutter
I'm told I have *photophobia*
which means
fear of light

maybe it is a fear of light because
being disabled in public is an anxiety
I wear sleep masks on the subway
LED brings aphasia and brain fog
I bark out gibberish at flashing bike lights
when they find the centre of my brain
that no longer can process them

I left school to work in lighting
let my life become theatres stadiums
film crews ballasts and trucks
1000 watts to 20,000 watts
from practical lights to xenon bulbs
that if dropped became actual bombs
they would take the actors off set
when we were placing one
into the head of the lamp

Photophobia: fear of light

how can I be diagnosed with fear
when I've risked my life for light
climbed the guardrails
while operating a crane at a hundred feet
to replace a white-hot scrim on a 18K
as a thunderstorm approached the movie set

as the ballast sat too close
magnetizing my very cells
and my old crew dies of ALS
and the producers still won't admit
how they got that disease

as I folded my knees into disability
inside a blizzard with a 10K
in a narrow crane bucket for
eight hours instead of fighting for
my rights

I've climbed on unregulated
A-frame ladders knowing they
were deemed too dangerous
as I've flown through the rafters
of a theatre that's never heard of
a harness

Photophobia: fear of light

I can tell you exactly why you feel that way
in blue-white light   why you forget your name
because a disco ball took it

why people only go to your restaurant once
because they remember the headache and not the meal
and why we'd first switch out all the fluorescents
before the camera even got there and
my body still knows how long I can touch hot metal
before it burns

I can tell you what's incandescent and what's LED
by the way my brain starts to sputter out
by how aphasia takes over mmmmmmmmmmmmy
momomamamaaaamouth and turns
it into reflexed mishmash of animal gibberish

I can tell you how I loved light so much I didn't
report the harassment I received
for being a femme-presenting tech
from the very first day
when I was assaulted by my mentor
in my high school theatre
till my last day working with men who
grabbed my breasts before asking my name
and called me *Mountain Dew* in the summer
because hey it was the 90s and all of them
could decide if I got to work or not

Photophobia: fear of light

years after this job I bury my husband and his sister
and I go right back to work
I spend a day with a flickering light
which turns my small migraine humming

into a full-scale hemiplegic
into something closer to a stroke into a numb face
and arm
a swirl of what words used to be and it's like a door
was left open that day and now all the light gets in

I used to think moths
were enamoured with light
now I know it traps them
interrupts their navigational systems
to the delight of prey
and they call that *phototaxis*

I didn't fear the harassment
or death or the level of danger
on every set or lighting booth or truck
all I did was never listen when they said
someone like me couldn't do the job

maybe I loved light so much
I became the moth

what do you call it
when your passion
becomes your disability?

please don't tell me
fear has anything
to do with it

Ham Sweat

If I were to take a giant ham
and carve a man out of it
it would look like you

your fingers sausage-thick
your brow a furrowed slab
your fat-lined nose plunging downwards
your bulging mouth
clown-sized

we meet outside your house
you ask me for something and I oblige
you grip me in a firm handshake and
your smell turns my palm ambrosial

your stench
your core
I want to bottle you
hand you over to perfumers
so they can scrape your skin
and share you

the world would turn into
an apocalyptic porno
hearts and hard-ons would burst
backs would break
pelvises would snap

your sublime smell
has me trolling past your door
trying
    vying
        dying
to shake that meaty cut of your hands again
so I can huff my palm
all the way home

somehow
I'm too shy to ask you if you are wearing something
but I think the answer to this question
will only be found
inside your careful bungalow
behind your retirement lawn
your polished knobs
and your wife's spoon collection

but I keep coming back to you
ignoring my old haunts
the gym the clubs the saunas
I even stop sniffing subway scents
though the days are stifled sweat

you see
I've found my aromuse
and it's not
Armani
    Ford
      Miyake
        or Klein

and true   some will call our
immense age gap indecent
but how long does it take to
make a man smell like that?
he probably spent the first thirty years
roiling in Aramis and mountain water
before creating a daily regime of
anointing himself in bacon grease
while eating chunks of cedar
soaking in tree sap
and drying his skin with saddle leather

then one day it happens
The End of Muse

an aura of braised meat pulls me to him
a handshake too long
a five-dollar bill
is pressed into my palm
he whispers his wants
wetly in my ear
I politely resist
but my wrist is grabbed so hard
that the blood to my fingers stops

I wrench away from intoxicating odours
it's over
my loss is five senses large
my grief is wrapped up in aromatic memory
like prosciutto

really
only five bucks?

That Time I Was Beaten Up at a Party, Circa 1992

I remember some night after the club shut and the next
party happened and I was sitting in a circle of smoke
and booze and some guy just flew into the room and
grabbed me pulled me out wordlessly into the hallway
and beat me up and the whole time I was thinking *maybe*
he's doing this because he thinks I'm hot and felt somehow
superior because no one ever really looked at me and
then he left to get coke and I came back into the room
no one looked at me and I wondered if I was just a ghost
now *did I die out there* but I didn't want sympathy or an
ice pack for my eye I just wanted someone to recognize
I existed when I wasn't giving a handjob or dancing in
a cage but how do you stand out when we were just all
becoming ghosts and statistics and sometimes people
say *don't you wish you could be young again* and I say *fuck*
no I can't even believe I survived the first time and I never lie
about my age because that's how I celebrate survival
because that was just a Wednesday night for us at the
Boom Boom Room

Lazy Tongue

For my childhood lateral lisp

Recess has barely started
and I'm hoping that you have already farted
because your butt is on my head
and I'm wishing myself invisible or at least dead

you see I wasn't raised to be your stool
but I can see how you think me a fool
because when I talk   I drool
and I stopped talking in my fifth new school

Class let's meet our new student   she's just a bit shy
she doesn't look up and she's dressed like a guy
honey why don't you tell us a little bit about yourself?

and I do but I avoid any *S*
words like *schtealth like schorry*
and *schtupid* and *schtop teasing me please*
like *don't aschk me more questionsch*
I am down on my knees
like *schick* and *embarrassched* and I know you'll
juscht teasche
like if I'm honey
you look like a *schwarm of beesch*

you see I have what's known as a lazy tongue
like all the other letters are running around

but the *S* is sitting on a bench looking glum

so every recess I find my bricked corner
and I sit there like my own designated mourner
and eventually the kids just stop talking to me   thankfully
until of course
you   came and sat on me

now I am praying like that holy school taught me
to God and Jesus and that beautiful chick Mary
that they could hear me that they could fix me
that they could even see me
sitting underneath the butt of this bully

but my God couldn't hear me
and my God couldn't fix me but
my God did invent (or so I was told)
speech therapy

I schell scheaschells by the scheaschore
and she schellsch scheaschells by the
scheashore

I'm sick to death of this flippin' chore
and I don't want to *"schell these schells"* anymore

But
I have all of these words that I just want to say
I have a million unspoken words everyday
and I'm tired of having my teachers speak to me slow

like this
is
how
quickly
I
think

like I'm a freak show because

my drool
could fill
a sink

this mouth makes me want to scream
I want to be the one who's mean
I want to read that chapter out loud
I want to gather a flippin' crowd
I want my spoken word to be a source of joy
and not to be squelched by the butt of this boy

so

I schell seashellsh by the scheashore
and sche schellsch seashellsch by the seashore

and I say this for an hour straight
every Monday and Thursday until grade eight
when they're not making me swallow
so much water I'm an ocean
just to teach this lazy tongue
a brand-new motion

those of you
who fight to be heard
to stumble and stutter
over mountainous words
who *schell seashellsch* until
the beaches are bare
with mouths full of marbles
and spit to spare

we
will always make sure we've got something to say
because we'll always think that you'd rather turn away

so my spoken word has this extra little trait
because this lazy tongue
is now
a heavyweight

SCAN TO HEAR THE MUSIC!!

Act II: All Horns and Drums and Triumphant Strings

Poems to Be Performed
with Music or Puppetry

Club Q

In loving memory of Daniel Aston, Kelly Loving, Ashley Paugh, Derrick Rump, and Raymond Green Vance.

> *To be performed with a loop of ukulele, foot tambourine, kazoo, musical saw, and random vocal sounds. It should have the feel of a pop tune.*

When I dance I am no one's gender
my knees do what I ask of them
my hips become wave pools
my hoodie up   my smile wide
my anxiety is handed trial
separation papers
don't worry baby, I'll be back

there is nothing like a queer nightclub
the abandon   the fashion   the celebration
the bartender everyone has a crush on
and after he has top surgery
he gets a crush on himself too

like a plucked hair
if you dare remove us
three more will show up
and I remember going to a memorial
for the Pulse nightclub shooting
and someone said *they can't*
kill us all and I came out trans
because I needed to live

we know that even in death
they will tell you how to grieve
and what your name used to be
they will call a trans woman a drag
queen and that's why we dance
because no one can tell us what
to do with our bodies when the
music drowns everything out

bullets don't stop our joy
when one is fallen we say their name
the name they told us
we say her pronouns
when she saves the fucking club
we say everyone's name but not
the killer's because no
one can dance to that shit

My Uterus Meets My Breasts in a Medical Waste Facility and They Go Out for Drinks to Talk Shit About Me

To be performed with puppets created out of nylons, red and blue yarn, and cotton to resemble my now-absent breast tissue and uterus. The puppets are worn as sleeves and their mouths are my hands in the nylons.

Though they've never
seen each other before
they know the language
of my vascular system

like roots of trees looking
to hold hands it takes them
some time to burrow through
the medical waste facility
and finally grasp arteries

Let's go get fucked up
my breasts bark out
they always liked a party

But wouldn't that thin our blood?
my uterus asks

When the hell did that ever stop us?
my breasts cackle
We'll get drinks for free!

tatas decree and
shimmy themselves into
underwire into push-up bra
then covered in camisole

ever connected to these wild orbs
my uterus gathers itself
sloppy with heavy walls and roiling fibroids
calls a cab and off they go

uterus starts to look for a quiet
booth for all to be encased in
ute loves feeling surrounded
they have always been a pack animal

That's not how to get drinks
breasts retort and through some
sort of physio-illogical miracle
they roll up a stool and plunk
themselves on the bar
immediately drinks are sent
a man slides over to talk
about his days as a quarterback
and breasts finally get tired and say
What colour are my eyes?

the man realizes he didn't notice
they weren't connected to anything
he screams and runs away

uterus curls into the barstool next to cleavage

finally at ease because
they have a rhythm unmatched once
connected

uterus takes a boob shot
starved for blood it hits ute quick
and they shout-ask
    What the fuck was all that

breasts heave then sigh
more drinks arrive
    You mean Charlie's surgeries?
asks breasts

    I can't believe he just got rid of us
spits uterus

    We were never appreciated
breasts announce and pour
boob shots all around

uterus sloppily declares
    I coulda given them babies
    they never even tried uteral orgasms

breast heave another sigh
more booze arrives another man
slinks over and also can't find their eyes
and boobs fake-whine
    All those times Charlie let men cum
    on me I was hoping to have my

own little breasts to love
and toss a shot on themselves
they ejaculate into laughter
fluid and matter fly everywhere

each shot makes them looser
which for tissue isn't good
They never wanted meeee
uterus cries making even more
of a puddle of itself

I blame the woke army
the breasts say
and the woke army buys
them another drink
and once asked
still can't find their eyes

The bartender calls me
tells me to come pick up
my parts
they're cut off

I send a cab for their safe return
to the medical waste facility
ask the bartender to hold up the phone
so I can read them this note:

Dear my old body parts

I know
you tried so hard
to make me feel whole
maybe
it would help to think
that this was me
loving you so deeply
that I set you free

I've Been Bleeding Since You Left Me

To be performed with slow harmonics on viola, layers of tense little swirls of sound.

The bleeding started before you left me
let's not be dramatic
dramatic like   how much can a body lose?
dramatic like   am I passing grief or clots?

dramatic like trans guy returns to the hospital
where they will treat him like a woman
because 'men' don't menstruate or experience
perimenopause even though 'men' is the
root of all of these words

this bleed started in May and it's almost September
maybe today I'll have to give into the rage of my body
the dread of my autoimmune blood disorder
has me doing daily triage
my skin more ghostly each day
breakup poems become lab requisitions
become Holter monitors and oximeters

in this bloody tide have been deaths and diagnoses
and masking still though they say the COVID party's over
and more deaths and strokes and
        I miss your laugh like platelets

like everything is out of focus and I sit more than I stand
like why am I the sickly brother in some Victorian novel
draping myself everywhere   staying low to the earth

bloody like yesterday my neighbour screamed at me that
god hates me and called me *fag*   like I wish these
were all metaphors but it's just sometimes

life is a slow trickle and sometimes it's clumps and
bursting bloody garbages I'm too tired to take out
like I know I should go to the hospital   but instead

I triage alone   monitor the tachycardia and lower eyelids
I used to work in this same emergency room
and I know what it's like to ignore
what you cannot change

I've been bleeding since you left me
it's not a metaphor but I miss what we had
like how my body misses my blood

3 Minutes in the Closet

To be performed with two loops. The first one is percussive, hand-clapping the beat to the tune "You've Lost That Lovin' Feelin'" by The Righteous Brothers. For the second loop, sing the phrase "you've lost that lovin' feeling" softly.

I have to throw my own party
to get my first kiss
pretend to find a bottle
    Oh what's this?
    should we play spin the bottle
    or maybe 3 mins in the closet?

it was a relief it was you Peter
the shy strawberry blonde
who slept with
his eyes open on school trips
the one who didn't push
anyone into corners

of course now I hope
you were gay too
that even
this moment
was a trans one

we spoke for the first
two mins of the three
stared at each other's lips

smooshed our faces together
tongues staying in respective mouths
it felt like a check mark
nothing like lust

back at school
my bullies dare me
to sing to you Peter
        You've lost that lovin' feelin'

and I do
I interrupt the ball game

you are on first base
            too fitting
I sang so loud
a spray of lisp sprung loose
but I didn't stop
I sang harder
sometimes
if you make them laugh
they won't beat you

and Peter you became
even more like a strawberry
a flush   a blush   a ripened fruit
as I posed like a proposing man
my knee on first

I transcended
into clown

into potential
into fearless

no one knows
what to do when power
is interrupted
when weird tomboy
becomes king
when the bullied
become
the show

Hey You Lucy Liu

To be performed in a public washroom alongside Lucy Liu, if she's available, and a full camera crew.

I first saw you onscreen in a gender-neutral washroom
all the lawyers shared in the legal drama *Ally McBeal*
circa 1998

you—a top-floor lawyer, a swan, a revelation

me—merely a gaze, an unseen audience
just a closeted transmasculine wondering why
every washroom wasn't like this

your sitcom unisex washroom
became my non-binary oasis
and you   all business suit and silk
blouse ready for chambers woke me
in ways I could never work out until
the cheap wine orgy years later

look Lucy Liu
our lives are messy
I—an endlessly self-centring people-pleaser
and you—a martial arts expert and multimedia artist

ok so I'm a multimedia artist too
do you mind if we talk when

we're in the gender-neutral stalls
during a closed set taping

my gender really took to you
it wanted to hold your
Hermès Birkin bag in *Sex and the City*
avenge your snow dreamy death in *Kill Bill*
show up for your New York art opening
offering a tiny plate of shrimp tartlets
a glass of Moscato and a laugh for your wit

OUR LOVE: Season 3, Episode 11
INT. WASHROOM – DAY

CHARLIE & LUCY *exit stalls, snap briefcases on the sink,*
share Blistex and take makeup off in a way that only
increases their power

CHARLIE (to LUCY)
You'd look so good as a man

LUCY *(raises eyebrow)*
Never as good as you babe

CHARLIE
(winks, straightens his tie, purr-growls into the mirror)

The thing about gender-neutral washrooms is
if you want to gawk at us   come to my girlfriend's art
opening in Tribeca
She likes a dry white I'll be saying in a satire-rich way

and behind my every grin
is a simple wish that after having
our history   language   and identities torn from our
lips   loves   and lives for hundreds of years

we could have
just one
fucking washroom
that's ours

Goldust, "The Bizarre One"

To be performed with light ukulele fingerpicking.

You said *yes* when Vince McMahon asked you to be
an androgynous wrestler   later looked it up
asked *what the hell did I get myself into?*

being the son of Dusty Rhodes means there's
a different ladder to climb   so you dipped
yourself in gold paint   played at being queer

as your wife turned masculine-manager
puffing on the fattest cigars
and further bending gender

you won matches by preying on homophobia
legitimized gay panic   molested wrestlers
in front of live and pay-per-view audiences you

  dry-humped a passed-out Undertaker
    stalked and assaulted Razor Ramon
      hid in a child's public washroom to scare R-Truth

Now in interviews you laugh
your homophobia older and sharper
brag about your idea to wear lingerie
to end the match against Rowdy Roddy Piper

snicker as you speak about the board meeting

where you pushed to get breast implants
when the WWE refused
did the phantom pain begin?

could you feel the gay wrestlers decide
to keep it in the closet for another season?
could you hear your crowds through their ears
as wrestlers stole makeup from your very face
holding it up as trophy   as triumph   as pelt?

did you get letters from us   the closeted many?
you were our only representation
did a trans girl hear the sounds of the screaming crowd
as proof that she was disgusting?
did she keep a razor blade in her pants as you did?

or are you like any other trans or non-binary person
aware you are a warning   a pawn   a weapon?
do you laugh through a life that doesn't feel like it's yours
feel the nostalgia of wrestlers' lips kissing in the ring
as a crowd of thousands chanted your name?

now in this absence
you try to change the past
loathing your character on podcasts
laughing in hoodies and hate
the shine stripped away

Goldust
did you know there's still time
to get those breasts you wanted?

do you ever dream
about how close you came
to truly being you?
slip back into that golden suit
lament your flat mannish chest?

Snow White Dreams

To be performed with singing from the original score from the 1937 movie Snow White and the Seven Dwarfs. *Open the poem by playing "Someday My Prince Will Come" on the musical saw, then drop the saw and start singing the part on the right-hand margin.*

Someday my prince will come…

Princess Snow White
my people call me
float hands over my translucent skin
make bedtime stories
of our true love tale

but what happens after
happily-ever-after?

Someday we'll meet again…

no one asks about the friends
who are snarled away from my door
who are the subject of every fight
ever since the prince
my husband
checked the unbloodied sheets
of the Royal Wedding Bed

I didn't think my lovers
                    my seven lovers
were big enough to 'take' my virginity
oh what a fool I was

their perfect sizes found me easily
climbed up my snow-white skin like surrender

my husband shoves mirrors in front of my face
calls me *the fairest of all the whores*
and I weep to placate him
but my tears belong to the seven pieces
of my bitten apple heart

I remember joy
a kitchen clanging with music and dancing
moments when Grumpy seemed more like Happy
cheers when Bashful would forget his own name
and Doc   oh Doc
he knew anatomy as if he'd built me

And off to his castle we'll go

castle mornings
the king's men march me from my marriage bed
to my happily-ever-after prison tower
my family calls me Princess in crowds
and an *Evil Witch* through the bars
of my sky-high cell
the guards
rain rotten apples down on me

I eat every bruised maggoty bit
wishing

I am wishing...

for thc bliss of poison

my love-song dwarves
have become tiny graves
mounds of relief
appear in His Highness's land

To be happy forever I know

this should never be a story spun sweetly
girls here think it's a gift
to be molested by handsome princes
while you slumber

but marrying the man
who stole your kiss
means you'll never sleep
deeply enough
to revisit
your
dreams

Altar Boy

To be performed while playing "Ave Maria" by Franz Schubert on the musical saw between stanzas.

I carry the Body of Christ onstage
a little plate with two wafers
I wonder what part of Jesus
is going into their mouths

I learn to kneel without fainting
I *ring the bells too loud* they say
I am always volunteering for funerals
they are during school hours

Ave ave ave Mariiii iiiiahh
I sing harmony a heavenly high
I think maybe Jesus will notice me
thank me for the banners I made

or maybe he's pissed I keep giving
his blood away feeding priests his
body holding up a gospel so big for
my small arms as they reframe him

three girls and I fought to be here
they say 'Altar Server' now
though something in me prefers 'Altar Boy'
breasts betray me and grow beneath robe

I lose my faith by grade eight but stay for feminism
my catholic school calls me *druggie* and
slut and *Satan*—at church I am cherished
the catholic women's league thanks me for fighting

it will be a decade before another girl
is allowed to be an altar server this was
part of the deal they say and hide us
when the bishop visits

church becomes a stage much like my gender
I am only here because it feels safer
because I need a place where I'm valued
because Jesus was also a radical

Meatmares

To be performed in the style of "Wicked Game" by Chris Isaak on ukulele and musical saw.

I wake on a greasy sheet
I'm haunted by sleep
you see it's the meat
it must be the meat because
if one tiny tasty bite
crosses my lips just one minute past the hour
of ten
I'll be dream fighting the faceless men
again
I'll be sweating and shaking and
soundlessly pleading for my husband to wake me
    baby please save me

you see it's the meat
I get meatmares
no   really
just look at these entries in my dream diary

swimming in a sea of bloated dead bodies
10:05 I ate sausage, turkey

being choked by a fleshy tree
10:30 veal scallopini

believe me
it must be fear enzymes passed from muscle to mouth

you cows were just chillin'
locked up atrophied in your pen
now you're nose-to-asshole marching
and ol' Bessy's up the plank
twitching and dying
and that fear?
it's mainlined
        your flatlines
                your final lines
                        your silent screaming

I wake my husband and I up
not so silently screaming
        you're dreaming
flops out of his mouth
his flat affect
the signs of neglect

he's stopped washing again
and last night after ten
I swallowed the dread
of an emptying pig pen

you see it's the meat
        it's the meat that's the problem
and the marrow it tells me such terrible things
like that he laughs at me
so cruelly

and maybe it's been telling him things too
because why else would he say to me
that *you control me by the way you walk*

(stop walking)

that *you breathe too loud*

(stop breathing)

that *you don't love me anymore*

(stop loving)

yet he needs me to stay
so that he can laugh at me
because he's no match
for what's left of my sanity

when I eat meat after ten
I get meatmares
and there's too much protein
and there's these protein strains in my husband's brain
and I wake up silently screaming
his name again
stuffed full of the Colonel's madness
he makes me a chicken

I say nothing of the stench
because when I do he makes
such gangrenous promises
like that he'll slaughterhouse himself
ever since his heart attack my husband
wishes he were a cold slab of meat

our eighteen-hour days of being a film grip and electric

makes downtime narcoleptic
I can't focus to see his food rotting on the floor
the mould the maggots and more
I try to convince my subconscious to stay
with a man who would rather slip away

I wake screaming on a greasy sheet
and every day he starts in again
and every night I eat meat after ten

because my heart
is full of nightmares
that tell me to keep loving
a man I can't talk with
            I can't walk with
                        I can't breathe with

his health is making me mental
and we got from happy to here
so gradually
because his health used to be so
much less mental

I eat meat late most nights
so that he'll believe me
that waking up next to what
you're becoming
isn't what's terrifying baby
you see it's the meat
it's the meat that's the problem

The City Wants

To be performed with a harmonica loop, low and slow like an ambulance, with a higher melody over top, on loop pedal.

The city
climbs into subways
files into stations
breathes into itself

the city is complacent in its
rejection of science
of feeble public health warnings
of something that dares slow it

the city wants your lungs
it wants your nervous system
all your dreams fogged by
its emulsion

the city has read your eyeball
and knows you are dreaming of
moving to the country
the city will spit you out

the city doesn't need us
it will be rebar and concrete
and nothing breathing that
isn't regulated and monitored

feed the city your children
give it your taxes your fingertips
scream at its unending injustices
coat it with the anxiety it causes

the city wants more concrete poured
another highway another condominium
rip more roots out of the earth clear the way
for more metal tubes of people racing

the city will win if we let it
the city will win if we let it
the city will win if we build it

This is For You Ry

To be performed with dulcimer and glass slide, after "Feelin' Bad Blues" by Ry Cooder.

My first apartment was
down the street from
a mile-high bridge
that had a rusted
catwalk underneath

I would climb onto this
crumbling vertebrae tightrope
and limp the length of it
listen to Texas blues
on my walkman as I teetered
and thrilled my acid-infested brain

those teenage times were
waking up to
what bit my ankles
long-haired losers sharing
my sofa bed and
bad teenage moves
leaving a school I
dropped out of while
dropping tabs
    surgery rehab
        codeine pills
            and fear-based thrills

Ry you might think this was me
at the crossroads of my own making
falling asleep behind the wheel of life
but it was also me trying to shake
myself awake after a knee surgery
that had me overdosing on
a mind-set I could not walk
away from because I literally
could not walk and once I could
I tried to defy gravity

and I understand it all now because
none of us even knew what
transmasculine was and those
were the days when gay only
meant AIDS and so didn't we
queer little kids all
start to death defy
as our mentors passed away

Ry how could you have known this
because your music held me closest
I would disappear into this song
such a melancholy drift
down some sweet-lipped river
each note numbing me further
drifting me away from myself
dipped in the syrup of a glass guitar slide

I used to make slides
out of smashed wine bottles
grind their snapped necks

on the pavement and
try at the guitar to sound
anything like you

Ry wouldn't it have been different
if I knew why I wanted my brain
to stay far from my body
for it to have no witnesses
I scurried it away from parental eyes
dangled it from bridges
fed it pills and booze and hallucinogens
hid it under other people

Ry you wouldn't believe
what I can do with ramen
and rice with soup base
and boiled potatoes please
don't stop playing to find
out the recipes really aren't worth it
and I was acting like
I was not worth it but dude

who needs high school when
teachers call you a stupid bitch
and openly stare at your tits
when it's all a haze anyways
and classmates kick your crutches
and name you cripple
and no one says they're gay

and migraines take your days
and break your brain and the

hash is too expensive but acid's not
and all that's left is ramen and
the occasional cheesecake
your roommate makes
and the graham cracker
crust box topples one day
becomes a shower of
cockroaches to envelop your
self-bruised body in
and even then it feels like
someone else's tragedy because
whose roach-covered body is this?

I live only a mile from this
old lifestyle and I see it in the eyes
of too many kids I teach Ry and
so I guess what I'm trying to say is

who did you listen to at the
bottom of the well because it sure
sounds like you were there
and sometimes youth will say
my art lifts them like yours did for me

Ry isn't that the greatest thing to hear
that you've created
the kind of art that
keeps lost people from

jumping off of bridges
and Ry isn't that
the best kind of thrill?

The Moon Was Lonely Last Night and Kept Me Up

To be performed while playing "Moon River," composed by Henry Mancini with lyrics by Johnny Mercer, on the musical saw.

The Moon was howling last night
as galaxy dust blew past
as a slow trickle of blood
fell from her eye
a sigh so broad
Jupiter stopped ringing

she inhaled my curtains
shattered the window
away from my face
I watched shards rise
towards atmosphere
then fall into a violence
puncturing the earth

sometimes she sings to me
a crater puckering
a halo of sounds encircle
other times she puts her
heated palm to my face
kissing me with each
light beam

I can't remember when
The Moon started talking to me
directly but I do remember
everyone leaving me
as I tried to tell them
about her voice and
how she makes love like
a million-year-old

so I keep quiet about it
and The Moon told me
she doesn't mind
this secrecy
but last night
I heard her sing the song
of an astronomical body
who had no lover
brave enough
to claim her

The Anatomy of the Cecil Hotel

To be performed as the voice of the hotel. Make loop pedal builds of elevator sounds, murmuring, and any other hotel sounds that seem necessary.

My guests arrive
enter through my toe
ride elevators
up my spinal column
sometimes they
make love in my ulna
fight in my fibula
become a clot of blood
in my vena cava

many have thrown open
my eyelids to leap
claw at my sides
as they realize
they want to live
on their way to death

I am a library
of human triumph and tragedy
each furnished crevice
houses stories of resilience
and complete defeat

I always have a vacancy
for those who wish
to hide from the world
just ring the bell
the ghosts will help
you to your rented
tomb

Le Pathétique

To be performed with the final symphony from Pyotr Ilyich Tchaikovsky, "Le Pathétique," as a backdrop, or build a loop of an orchestra warming up with layers of tuning the viola.

In grade six my catholic school
music teacher told us
that this symphony
was your suicide note

hence the name
"Le Pathétique"
which translates from French to
English as
"The Pathetic"

The original title was
your mother tongue Russian
"Pateticheskaya"
which translates to
"The Passion"
but no one wanted to celebrate
a gay man's passions in 1893

high society hid your male lovers
and asked to meet your wife
I wonder if the crescendos
in "Le Pathétique" are the climax

cries of your boyfriends
who draped themselves over divans
as you played your piano
these loves in your arms hidden from
your country
        your time
                your marriage

handlers combed through your letters
before they called the coroner
wrung out gay desire from your sheet music
told stories of how you boldly drank
unboiled water during a cholera outbreak
at an elite restaurant
and it was this   your bravado
that was your undoing
but what fine restaurant would
knowingly put poison in your hands?

we queers see you Pytor
we can hear your triumph
feel the fanfare of an oboe's lipped lover
the teased swirl of a French horn
the percussion section an undulation of bed frame
notes embracing every inch of rugged skin

Tchaikovsky
I'm sorry to say that little has changed
in Mother Russia
that the world stands idle
as Chechnya sends queers

to concentration camps
but they will never stop our joy
or how us gays
will always find the truth of you
all horns and drums and
triumphant strings

they called your passion a suicide note
so that no one would question
how you died
but we queers know
what murder
sounds like

Inside Vitreous

An ekphrastic poem in response to Serkan Özkaya's "ni4ni v.3" *as performed at his installation at MOCA in Toronto, Canada. The room contained a seven-foot mirrored sphere. The gallery walls were painted to be reflected onto the sphere as though it was a giant eyeball.*

To be performed with viola interludes between stanzas.

I was in a lethal band van
careening over the Prairies
on the way to the next gig
the first time I felt
the eye of the creator

I've been naked
in many public spaces
felt eyes memorize
even experienced the power
of audience averting such overtness

but when I was travelling
over ironed-flat
depressed endlessness
I felt my most disgusting
a dung beetle interrupted
inspected by relentless
eye in the sky

it dissolved through tour clothes
sunk through skin
seeped through bone
massaged its way into marrow

what I know now but
couldn't perceive then is that
whatever name you have
for that eye in the sky—know
that creators love their artwork
each human
a myriad of mistakes
and celebrations

don't you remember?
how things that used to scare you
became strengths?
that shame slinked out
every door you showed it through?

sclera is not veined maps for
where it all went wrong
but a glory of how you've survived
the creator's eye knows that
here is where you fell
here is where their fear became
yours and here is where
you tossed it out the
band van window

you cannot lie
when your creator is watching
so live my friends
let your flaws rise to the surface
for they too require sunshine

make a promise now
that you will never stop
growing learning and recovering
under the eye of the first being
that loved you

I Think Love Songs Should Leave Me Alone

To be performed with a whimsical ukulele riff on loop.

Oh love songs how you let me down
how you got me to thinking
I could change people
that making everyone
feel better than me
would make me
feel
better

but here I sit in
pyjamas unwitnessed
ignored dating apps
patting someone else's dog
and no one's rings
but my own

love songs you make me sad
with the yearnings   oh
the melodic yearnings
you take me to
the places
memories
should be left

maybe the only good songs are ones
where your exes hold on and maybe
I'm the borrowed dog here
so loyal so ready for another
reason to sit by my lover's side
lick their hands

listen up love songs
it's time to stop messing with me
I have been you a few times
and I get it I so get it
I do everything for love
I really do

I just wish sometimes
love songs
wouldn't be
so moving
so shimmy
and shake

but damn
don't you sound good
love songs

Act III:
The Nothing to Lose

Poetic Monologues for Audition

Things I Took From my Hospital Jobs

Monologue for: Any gendered or agender person.

From: No One's Special at the Hot Dog Cart

Setting: Actor performs a spoken word piece directly to audience. Keep the title of the poem in the monologue.

Band-Aids
pens
lanyards
a stained set of scrubs
and the ability to laugh like a siren
when tragedy wants to win

gauze
Steri-Strips
gloves
and the knowledge that time
is meant for love

paper clips
stories I cannot share
and the memories of how
we held each other through them

working in emergency is all reaction
so my art becomes prevention
dealing in death taught me

how to live
because I know that someday
I may only be a body
defined by need
level of infection
and semi-private
or private insurance
and I will enter that hospital knowing

I chased
my joy
when I could

Ode to Victor

Monologue for: Trans men, transmascs, and gender non-conforming and non-binary actors.

From: Mel Malarkey Gets the Bum's Rush

Setting: This is Mel's 'Male Impressionist' act as Victor the Crooner, but let's face it, Mel, she's really Victor, a trans man. In this scene, he is changing from Mel's last costume into being Victor in a suit. He alternates his voice from Mel to Victor. He starts with Mel's feminine voice.

When Hollywood
asked me for my list of characters
I included you   Victor

Victor   they laughed at you
they said there was no need
for me to ever dress as a man again
didn't I know that you're an aberration?

Hollywood said
we'll find you a leading man
Mel Malarkey you be
the beautiful woman you are

but Victor   how do I give you up?
that feeling I get when I

receive an audience like a gentleman
why would anyone want to
extinguish the swooning croon
stifle your gracious and delectable tone
the sharp shoes
the cufflinks like a brandished accent

how do you throw away
the greatest man you've ever met?

they've informed me you're dangerous Victor
but we know all about that
those evenings I started out as you crooning tunes

> *(sings "I Wanna Be Loved By You" by Herbert Stothart and Harry Ruby for a few bars, continues in Victor's voice)*

And they'd seek me out
the women who knew but didn't care
lined up outside this dressing room door
those cards flirted into our pocket

invitations from the dames who'd dare
or from gentlemen tired of their own costumes

they call me
    The Awakener
The Cake Eater   The Gigolo

I've grown used to
the bleating venom cries of terrified men

the slapping sound of pursuing wingtips
the pelted names that ricochet off alleyway walls

and those nights
when I would be swooned off stage
in the arms of a lover   or a customer
sometimes   depending on the fame or
frame of the dame
we would pass unnoticed

but when we walked with men who loved me
or women who showed their shame
why that's when the punishments would come

what a relief it must be
when anger is your parasite
to find a man like me

but it was all worth it every bloodied lip
every busted bit   because we took it like a man

(back in Mel's voice)

Victor   as brutal as you make my life you're a comfort
a haunting I'd never exorcise
you answer the question of *who am I*
with sifting whispers of *you look so handsome*
you make sweet the act of erasing my name

Victor   every time I am you
it's me telling the world *I am happy*

Ode to an Elegant Elephant Lady

Monologue for: Trans men, transmascs, and gender non-conforming and non-binary actors.

From: Mel Malarkey Gets the Bum's Rush

Setting: Victor reads this love poem in the green room of the Vagabond Theatre.

Dear sweet Ella Sue
when they first introduced me to you
your puzzling body was covered in a cape
there was a manager who kept you harnessed shackled
and shamed
he spoke for you
called you *Ella Fat Lady the Elephant Lady*
and your costume showed me only your eyes
two wishful windows surrounded by
your beautiful opera of a body
that grew despite your high-pitched nightly prayers

for once
I introduced myself as Victor
and you said my name
as if we'd woken up
still tasting each other
I asked you for your true name too
and your voice went tiny and confused saying Ella Sue?
it's hard to remember

something the world has taken from you
if bravery had a body
it would have been yours
the Elephantitis gave you gorgeous girth
stroked the muscle out of your frame
wrapped it in flesh that seemed to multiply
as I gazed at you

you cabinet of curiosities
each part of you another glorious effort
a delight

your brow a plump croissant
your arms like boas feeding on cats
your legs like knotted tree trunks
the tumours seemed to be fists pushing out of you
gnarled bumps of *you'll never be as tough as me*

and as strong as you were Ella Sue   you were twice
as sweet
you feeder of ducks   holder of dreams
dresser of wounds
even when corrected you called me Victor
and I grew to love you like an oasis

sweet Ella Sue
you made a gentleman of me and a gentler man of me
somehow your body always knew you were to be
a fiddle player
your hands kept dainty
the crooks of your elbows tumour-free

you were an impossibility
crowds fell in love with you   but not like me

dear sweet Ella Sue
you weren't long for this earth were you
for as your girth surpassed expectations
and your body was pulled into separations
you never lost sight of
how huge your heart could be

and when it finally burst
you fell into that big sleep beside me
I awoke to the chill of your body
once the heat of our home
all the ways you could love me
as me   as the man in me
and the woman in you   Ella Sue

nowadays I only really laugh when I think of your sass
and I still see you in our funhouse glass
though you've passed
know I still have the joy you gave me
and the heart of an elephant
beating inside of me

Veasons Vor Vhy I am a Total Tramp

Monologue for: Transmascs, transfemmes, non-cis women, sex workers, and gender non-conforming and non-binary actors.

From: Mel Malarkey Gets the Bum's Rush

Setting: Victor performs his impression of Marlene Dietrich for Mel's Audience at the Vagabond Theatre. He attempts a German accent.

Und now: Veasons, vor vhy, I'm a total Tramp

because I'm amazing
because you called me zat
because
like most prostitutes   quiffs and hookers
I too am a giving   empathetic
and generous person

because PROPAGANDA IS POWER!

because you calling me zat
is just another vay of saying
business-owning dame
who refuses to be tame

because men vork hard for zeir money
but women are expected to give work avay
like charity   like a dessert tray

because for a moment
vhen legs were bent
skin trampoline taut
your breath a skittering violin bow
your eyes became sky and sunshine spilled
from your mouth and you were happy
und zen blamed me—TRAMP!

because I'm full of joy—TRAMP!
because I call myself Tramp first
so zat it can drown out
the vays you get that vord so vrong

you see
Tramp used to mean
someone who lived on the lam
jumped boxcars on trams
knew zat vealth could be found
vithout an ounce of scratch
but living free
is as shunned as adultery

TRAMP!
because you forgot my name
TRAMP!
because I didn't vant to know your name
TRAMP!
because you threw everything else at me
and vords stay after bruises leave
and you never vanted to lose me

because powerful
boozy burlesque bodies are shameless
and you get paid more to vear less
because in-de-pen-dance
because smoke and lights and
straps and snaps
and heckles
vhy zey can also sound like claps

TRAMP!
Well auf wiedersehen

because maybe you zink I owe you sex
since I vrote this number

if I vrote about baking
vould I owe you pie?

but believe me
in this short human life
if you dare vrap yourself
around every joy to be had
taste peaches at too many fruit stands
part too many vays and too many legs
you too
can be called *TRAMP!*
and you know
vhen you give zis much
people vill take your name

but dahlings
Tramp just means good company
because zere is beauty in how
ve Tramps take care of others
and I like other generous
free-villed   hard-vorking people
am called *TRAMP!*

and if you've never been called zat before
vhy zen you're probably
not
          as nice
                    as me

Medusa's Serpent Speaks

Monologue for: Trans women, femmes, women, cis women, gender non-conforming and non-binary actors, and opera singers.

From: Medusa's Children

Setting: One of the serpents from Medusa's famous head of hair addresses the audience.

I thought men wanted to be rock hard
isn't that the centre of every war
isn't that why Medusa was punished for chastity
isn't that why she was cursed for saying no
now look at me
just a lock of what I used to be

I am what's left of Medusa
she was just a simple Gorgon
dedicated to worship in Athena's temple
to remain chaste despite what men wanted
Poseidon didn't like her no and took her
jealous Athena made her mortal   a thing to kill
and Perseus stole her head for a prize

her babies   Pegasus and Chrysaor
born of murder   birthed out of severed neck
think their mother a monster   a weapon

ask yourself this Perseus
what is it to be raped into existence
was that the poison in your brain?
we all know your father is Zeus
and your mother was forced
how sad this normality
that here in Greece
rape is considered godlike behaviour

Medusa's sweet children
may you be better   dear loves
may you find the strength of your mother
rather than the cowardice of your father

Euryale Reads Medusa's Letter

Monologue for: Trans women, women, femmes, cis women, gender non-conforming and non-binary actors, and opera singers.

From: Medusa's Children

Setting: Medusa's family gathers to listen to the reading of Medusa's long-buried letter by her older Gorgon sister Euryale.

A letter from my sister Medusa

Sisters
I hope you never have to read this letter
and instead have lived with me and had
many a moment of joy
anything but this feeling of doom
ever since Poseidon defiled me

maybe we would laugh about
this old thought that I
was to be killed for Poseidon's sins
the anxieties that his attack left me with

> the teeth-skittering silences
> filled with the eyes of men
> the cloud of a breath outside window
> how often the sea shouts my name

how I sense men are waiting for me
my body already in their fists
what have I done but be kind and chaste?
what have I done but be devoted to Athena?

sisters if you have found this letter
and I have been murdered as I suspect
I ask you to seek my babies
those kicks I feel inside
am I carrying more of his sons?

let them be raised to be different
let them know how to be lovable
that kindness is the best strength
that you can be your own music

Stheno and Euryale Speak of their Sister Medusa

Monologue for: Trans women, femmes, women, cis women, gender non-conforming and non-binary actors, and opera singers. This could be performed as a single voice audition.

From: Medusa's Children

Setting: Medusa's Gorgon sisters defend her memory. To be performed with dulcimer and musical saw on loop pedal and harmonic vocal effect.

STHENO :
Our sister deserved being defended
especially by the goddess to whom she
dedicated her simple life
Athena   your jealousy had you take the side
of our sister's rapist Poseidon
who thought Medusa more beautiful
so you made her
made her a thing to kill

but we
unlike our mortal sister
cannot be murdered
so we tell everyone the truth
of who is the danger   the warning
the ugly

EURYALE :
My sister Medusa
the dewed honey of her gaze
how could you make it poison?

STHENO :
Why must men
think we are here to take?
I watched my sister walk
up to Athena's court and a dread
set its tentacles into my heart
I knew then she was never to return

EURYALE :
Did you know my sister Medusa
would trace words into hot springs?
that she was the best at spitting
pomegranate seeds into kraters?
that rainstorms made her cry?
that they have since I held her as a baby?

STHENO :
What is it to be immortal and
to know your sister can die?
that you'll never have rest from that grief?
how do you love anyone?

what is it to become a fear?
a slow slide of claw to spine?
at the sound of your name Medusa

EURYALE :
Our sister's smile fed a town one time
it brought a baby calf to life, I swear
how could you interrupt magic, Poseidon?
how could you call yourself goddess, Athena?

Pegasus's Aria

Monologue/aria for: Agender, gender non-conforming and non-binary actors, and opera singers.

From: Medusa's Children

Setting: Pegasus addresses their family. To be performed with a viola build on loop pedal.

My aunties
I dream of mother
and the men tell me it's nightmares
there are children scared to sleep
for the image of what my mom became
a haunt   a threat   a warning

mother Medusa calls to me
when I am in the deep dreaming
asks me where her head is
she knows it to be missing
stolen for weaponry
tethered to the shield of her murderer
the winged-footed shame called Perseus
who once done with her
threw my mother's head into the sea

I have nothing to lose
I am born to be alone
there is no other Pegasus

is it my name
my breed
the name for something
not male or female?
because I feel like neither
and what I do feel
is other

my own brother   Chrysaor
denounces mother every day
pledges to the shrine of her murderer Perseus
shouts at the ocean for his father Poseidon

what is it to worship
the rapist of your own mother?
to call him any kind of father?

where is the womb of my mother?
the only place I never knew threat
my first home is a tomb
dear sweet Medusa
a beauty interrupted
the only Gorgon of her kind

we are the lonely
the nothing to lose

Daughter of Geppetto: Part I

Monologue for: Trans men, transmascs, and gender non-conforming and non-binary actors.

From: Daughter of Geppetto

Setting: This scene begins months after Pinocchio has saved his father from the belly of the dogfish. The musical backdrop is Nocturne Opus 9 No. 2 *by Frédéric Chopin.*

When the woodsman handed me to you Geppetto
back when I was just a talking log
I knew only one thing to tell my creator
my new father
that
I'm to be a real boy

and Geppetto though you heard me you flexed your jaw
and whittled me into your wish for a daughter
named *Pinocchia*

Father
isn't life a funny tide
when I was washed into the belly of a shark
one so big it swallowed your whole ship
and I found you eating the fish
that clapped at your feet

you grinned a shine of scales
and cried out
                    Pinocchia!

I should have been full of mirth
for I had thought you dead for years,
but what came out of my mouth was

No Father   it's me
your son   *Pinocchio*

and I waited
for that old rage
the one that called me sick
called me devil   called me daughter
that shouted me from our little hut

but you smiled as if you had to make room
for six rows of teeth   greeted me *Pinocchio?*
and it was then I saw what living in
the belly of a shark can do to a person

Father Geppetto
you suffer a softened mind   remember little
and can be convinced of anything

this is our true story

sometimes Father
back when I slept at your feet
I would beg the Fairy to change me into a soft thing

something never to be named
only loved and held like your blanket
or your pillow

Father I heard that after I left you became the town's
grim tale
a wearied frenzy   a voice that slapped the sides of houses
demanding your daughter
                                        Pinocchia
be returned

you should have looked for me instead
I told you my name before I left

this morning
as I cut your nails
you asked me had I written another chapter
in the story of our lives
                                        The Adventures of Pinocchio
how was it coming?

Father
I write it only when you are asleep
I walk out into the woods
so as to not shatter the windows
with the menace of birds that arrive
their beaks thirsty to erase this lie of a nose
that winds and curls as I create the story
that I wish was ours   one where you always
called me *son*

what a deep vertigo you are in Father
and I'm ashamed that it brings me peace
to never hear you call me
                                        Pinocchia
again

and Father thank you
I hear your prayers each night
asking the Fairy to turn me into
a real boy before you die

but that old wish means nothing to me now

yesterday
you held me and said,
                                        Pinocchio
                                        you are such a fine son
                                        such a good lad

Father this is all I've ever needed
to feel real in your eyes

my name is Pinocchio
and this
this is our true story

Daughter of Geppetto: Part III

Monologue for: Transmen, transmasc, and gender non-conforming and non-binary actors.

From: Daughter of Geppetto

Setting: Pinocchio remembers his first friend, Lamp-Wick. To be performed with a dulcimer, and a dancer as Lamp-Wick in silhouette.

Lamp-Wick today I wrote our chapter
unearthed the boast of you   the brazen
the brawn   the ruckus of us

though you once knew me as Geppetto's daughter
you still asked me to join you and the other boys
on the caravan heading to the Land of Toys

sometimes when I dream we are
once again bright morning vines wrapped around each other
entwined in fairground fields full of wine and nectar
and you ask me if it's ok that you want to kiss the boys
and I hope you're talking about me

my dear Lamp-Wick
I know you feared the wild boys as I did
for we both hid so loudly around them

showed them our brute   our fearless   our cruel
but together   we were tender

Lamp-Wick
the things I said to make sure they never thought
me anyone's daughter
how many times I disparaged the
woman with the azure hair
the Fairy who had nothing
but kindness for me
just to be called brother
I called her such dreadful things

Lamp-Wick
you could have told the lost boys about me
turned this wooden body into
a wall of flame and smoke
for you to hide behind
you knew I would never betray you
so I wonder
if we had not become donkeys
and sold to different fates
could we have fallen in love
can we still?

or are we too haunted by that last day
where we spun country dances
laughing until we started to bray
and hooves grew from our feet
and our very bones shifted

and we galloped back to find
a stampede of horrors
each donkey the face of a wild boy
on Sundays I go to the market square
when they bring in the livestock
for sale or slaughter
look for the home of your eyes

I know you are alive Lamp-Wick
I would have felt the loss of you
my friend   I promise
I will not allow myself to grow back into
the ground until I find you once again

Daughter of Geppetto: Part IV

Monologue for: Transmen, transmascs, and gender non-conforming and non-binary actors.

From: Daughter of Geppetto

Setting: Pinocchio discovers that his father, Geppetto, has passed away. To be performed with viola on a loop pedal. This also works with layering whispers and voices to create the sounds of trees speaking to each other.

Father Geppetto
if I were human this is where I'd
say goodbye to you

but because I am made of earth
of water   of wood
I will instead introduce you to my first family
they've agreed to have you grow with them
for you to have a life with them

I have told them how sweet you have become
how illness has healed us
they want to embrace you so that we will always
have a home together
Father what a love you will know

(slow build of viola or vocals on loop)

I will bury you in no box Father
make room in the earth for them to
wrap you in tendrils
there is a lattice of roots that talks all day
in this forest
my first home is attached
to every hope of dirt
every green stick growth

come   hear the cry of each leaf
as it breaks from branch
await its glorious fall to forest floor
where it is welcomed back

(add another viola or vocal loop)

Father
I will bury you next to the tree from
where I was extracted
there is a little new branch
that sounds just like me
soon you'll hear them

it was a deep violence that was my beginning
and for a while I forgot this home
thought I could be just boy
that the Fairy could make me whole
but I had a serenity that needed no names

Father I know it is the sea that beckons you back
by the way you can never control the tide of you in sleep

your moans a whale call   how you always moved as if
our little hut might open its mouth and dive for supper

(add another viola or vocal loop)

but this forest knows our story best
it will send your regrets to the deep
it was always my nature to love you back
into the earth

sometimes Geppetto
when I missed my family too much
I would dig and burrow into their bosom
put a root on my tongue
just to hear their whisper

Father soon you will hear the songs of my brethren
the deep bass of a hollow oak
The sweet hum of lichen on beechwood bark
each celebration of sunshine on cypress

(stop track so there is total silence)

will you sense my homesickness Father
hear how lonely the earth is for me
since I was severed from trunk
nothing makes me feel more human
more like a real boy
than the ache of   silence

(start track back up)

Geppetto I promised you our story would be shared
The Adventures of Pinocchio!
I've signed the book *Carlo Collodi*
there's a publisher for it Father
they'll call it fiction so that I might have peace

Geppetto I'm so happy for you to see where
I truly came from
that you will experience
a love where you are enough
for I have always known
what it is to be cherished   to be held
by a family who only needs me
to grow with them

I wonder who will you become
with all that love
and freedom

Notes on the Monologues

"Things I Took from My Hospital Jobs" is taken from *No One's Special at the Hot Dog Cart,* which debuted at Theatre Passe Muraillc (Toronto) in 2024.

This solo show is framed around the story of 'Frank', a man who stalked me at my hot dog cart. I was a late-night hot dog vendor in Downtown Toronto in the early 90s and I learned a lot about how to de-escalate, and also to appreciate street communities. These skills evolved as I later became a 911 operator for ambulance, an emergency room worker, and hospital bed allocator. The show is filled with music, storytelling, and spoken word.

"Ode to Victor," "Ode to an Elegant Elephant Lady," and "Veasons Vor Vhy I Am a Total Tramp" are taken from *Mel Malarkey Gets the Bum's Rush*, which debuted at The Theatre on King (Peterborough) in 2015. It was later recorded as an album, *Mel Malarkey, Ode & Acts*, with Micheal Oesch, Beach Digital Media, in 2017

This solo vaudeville show is set in 1931. It's the last night at Mel Malarkey's Vagabond Theatre. She can't bear to tell the audience the news so she keeps the show going, bringing on ridiculous acts, and having her poetic goodbyes backstage (which is onstage). Mel Malarkey is also Victor the Crooner, a trans man who is losing the only place he could be applauded for who he is.

"Medusa's Serpent Speaks," "Euryale Reads Medusa's Letter," "Stheno and Euryale Speak of their Sister Medusa," and "Pegasus's Aria" are taken from *Medusa's Children*, a full length libretto commissioned by OperaQ and composed by Colin McMahon, which debuted as an opera film in 2021.

Medusa's final letter has been found, hidden in Athena's court. Her sisters, Stheno and Euryale, gather to read it out with Medusa's children, Chrysaor and Pegasus. Themes of family, loss, sexual violence, and toxic masculinity are told through a trans and queer lens.

"Daughter of Geppetto: Part I," "Daughter of Geppetto: Part III," and "Daughter of Geppetto: Part IV" are taken from *Daughter of Geppetto*, which debuted at The Emergency Performance Festival #22 with Public Energy Performing Arts in 2018, and featured choreographer / dancer Wes Ryan.

In this re-imagining of *Pinocchio* by Carlo Collodi, Pinocchio is a transmasculine character who was originally carved to be a daughter named 'Pinocchia'. The show begins after the rescue of Geppetto from the horrible dogfish where he was trapped for years. Pinocchio is happy his father cannot recall he ever carved him into a girl, but it's complicated because he's also aware his father's mind and body are weak. It is a story of grief, family, identity, and queer love.

I left "Daughter of Geppetto: Part II" out of the collection, because some things are best experienced rather than written.

Notes to the Poems

"Good News," "Hey It's Me, Your Closet," and "Photophobia" were published in *periodicities* in 2024.

"Trans March 2022" was published online as winner of *Arc Poetry Magazine*'s Arc Award of Awesomeness in 2022.

"Ham Sweat" was published online in Brick Books' Brickyard as a spoken word audio-poem in 2018.

"Lazy Tongue" was published as a video poem in *Ascending Aspirations* in 2012.

"This is for you Ry" was written to be a part of Mashed Poetics, a poetry and music show that matches songs with poets, created by RC Weslowski and Trevana Spilchen.

"Le Pathétique" was published in *CV2*'s issue 43.3 in 2020.

"Things I Took from My Hospital Jobs" appeared on the TTC as part of Poems In Passage in 2025.

"Ode to an Elegant Elephant Lady" was published in Capturing Fire Press's *Super Stoked: An Anthology of Queer Poetry from the Capturing Fire Slam & Summit* in 2028.

"Daughter of Geppetto: Part I" was published in Guernica Editions' anthology *Changing the Face of Canadian Literature* in 2020.

Acknowledgements

I have been blessed with so many amazing artists in my life, who support and influence my work. I would like to thank Lillian Allen, who has been such a trailblazer for spoken word, and has made sure we are recognized in the same arenas as more traditional poetry. Thank you to the theatres who believe in my work like Theatre Passe Muraille, The Theatre On King, Public Energy Performing Arts, and Buddies in Bad Times Theatre for helping me to build spoken word theatre projects and create platforms and workshops for others to shine. Thank you to Sheri-D Wilson for all you've done to create legacy in Spoken Word. Love to OperaQ for commissioning *Medusa's Children*, to Colin McMahon for composing, and Lauren Halasz for directing the opera film. Thank you to theatre collaborators Autumn Smith, Donna Michelle St Bernard, Wes Ryan, Sze-Yang Ade-Lam, Kate Story, Ryan Kerr, Janice Lee, and Adam Lazarus. To my poet workshoppers Alessandra Naccarato, Jacob Scheier, Lisa Richter, Alisha Kaplan, and especially my editor, Sonnet L'Abbé, we are forever in a band together my friend.

A big thank you to my family who has embraced me as Charlie, and how your growing acceptance is giving me so much more freedom. Not having knowledge around trans identities affected us all. Love to David Bateman for doing an original edit of this manuscript, and being such a performance beacon to me. To friends like Cat Schembri, Apanaki Temitayo, Nicole Russel, Pat Walsh, RC Weslowski, and Max Carney for your support always. Big love to Glad Day Bookshop for being a huge community heart. Queer lit helps us find each other, and ourselves. Big love to Phoenix The Fire for the Deaf performance art you brought to our videos. Thank you to the Writers Trust of Canada and to Dawson City for giving me time, space, and support to work on this manuscript.

Gratitude to Alayna Munce, Brenda Leifso, Manahil Bandukwala, and everyone at Brick Books for your continued support of my work and the lovely ways you show up. Thank you to the Ontario Arts Council and the Canada Council for the Arts for your support. Big love to Andrea Thompson who inspired this manuscript's focus. Respect to my trans and non-binary ancestors who paved the way, and to the youth, who will always expect more safety and support than I can ever imagine. Big love to the poetry slam community, especially to Toronto Poetry Project, who helped me grow as an artist, and for the opportunities you all give me to help bring in the spoken word playwrights of the future. May we never stop dreaming of all poetry can be.

Love always to my bands The Silver Hearts, Wine With Everything, Thunderfuck Berzerker, and my first theatre, the Union Theatre, for always being so punk and experimental. Finally, to my forever collaborator, Emmie Tsumura—you will always inspire me and I am so grateful for you being a part of this and every art project we get to devour.

More art more art more art.

Charlie Petch (they/them, he/him) is a disabled/queer/trans-masculine multidisciplinary artist who resides in Tkaronto/Toronto. A poet, playwright, dramaturg, librettist, musician, lighting designer, and host, Petch was the 2017 Poet of Honour for the speakNORTH national festival, winner of the Sheri-D Golden Beret Award from The League of Canadian Poets (2020), and founder of Hot Damn It's a Queer Slam. Petch is a touring performer, as well as a mentor and workshop facilitator. Their debut poetry collection, *Why I Was Late* (Brick Books), won the 2022 ReLit Award, and was named "Best of 2021" by *The Walrus*. Their film with OperaQ, *Medusa's Children*, premiered in 2022. They have been featured on the CBC's *Q*, were the Writer-in-Residence for Berton House (2023), and were longlisted for the CBC Poetry Prize in 2021. Their solo show *No One's Special at the Hot Dog Cart* debuted at Theatre Passe Muraille in 2024.

Colophon

Infinite Audition was designed by Emmie Tsumura in June 2025, on Treaty 13, Tkaronto/Toronto.

The typeface used throughout the book is Dante MT, designed by the German-born typographer and master printer Giovanni Mardersteig in the mid-20th century. During WWII, he was known to help political refugees find safety on other continents and published anti-Nazi sonnets through his own press.

The cover was designed in collaboration with the author, using imagery from Charlie's poetry. Each object holds a sacred world of wisdom in itself, and together in grief and celebration, they gather in this infinite audition.